KU-304-268

The Fundamentals of
Hospitality Marketing

C265918

Also available:

Principles of Hospitality Law, 2nd edition: Boella and Pannett

Informative Writing, 2nd edition: Goddard

The Tourism Development Handbook: Godfrey and Clarke

Passing Exams: Hamilton

Sales and Service for the Wine Professional: Webster

Using Computers in Hospitality, 2nd edition: O'Connor

Dissertation Skills for Business and Management Students: White

The Fundamentals of Hospitality Marketing

Steve Mawson

CONTINUUM
London and New York

To Mags and the Opuses

CHICHESTER COLLEGE
OF
ARTS, SCIENCE & TECHNOLOGY

CHICHESTER COLLEGE

Class. | Acc. No.

WITHDRAWN

FROM LIBRARY | C265918

ISBN 0 8264 4832 1

Continuum
Wellington House
125 Strand
London WC2R 0BB

370 Lexington Avenue
New York
NY 10017-6503

© 2000 Steve Mawson

All rights reserved. No part of this publication may be reproduced or transmitted in any form or by any means, electronic or mechanical, including photocopying, recording, or any information storage or retrieval system, without permission in writing from the publishers or their appointed agents.

First published 2000

British Library Cataloguing-in-Publication Data
A Catalogue record for this book is available from the British Library.

ISBN 0-8264-4832-1

Typeset by Ben Cracknell Studios
Printed and bound in Great Britain by Martins the Printers, Berwick upon Tweed

Contents

List of Figures

Preface

This book is for students who need to undestand the fundamentals of marketing in the hospitality industry, the principles of which parallel those of other service-related vocational areas of leisure and tourism.

Students are under increasing demands to acquire and familiarize themselves with knowledge and understanding of business disciplines, and marketing is arguably one of the most important. No matter how good the quality of hospitality products and service, no matter how precise the financial controls and how skilled and efficient the employees are, the whole operation is meaningless unless customers are prepared to part with their money – and the key to unlocking their wallets and purses is Marketing.

The book is divided into three sections, matching the model of marketing in Figure 1.2. Within each section is a series of chapters explaining the processes involved. Some have introductory vignettes, which are either born of fictional constructs, drawn from a range of experiences, or which are true, except that names and locations have been changed in order to protect the anonymity of the people involved.

Section A considers what the customer wants and deals with market research, competitors and costs.

Section B is concerned with developing the product and/or service to match the identified needs of customers established through market research, and on developing the correct marketing mix.

Finally, Section C examines the various methods of promotion.

Practitioners will find it helpful, in understanding the rationale behind what many intuitively do, to compare their own marketing 'tool kit' with the examples given.

Acknowledgements

The content, shape, design and structure of this book owe much to the contributions, some unwittingly provided, from the 'broad church' of the hospitality industry.

A special word of thanks to Jean and Karen for typing the initial chapters and to the incomparable Diane Smith, whose patient interpretation of my handwriting and amendments brought it all together.

Steve Mawson

SOME DEFINITIONS

Marketing is:

Effective customer value management

The delivery of a standard of living

Looking at the business through the eyes of a customer and organizing it to meet their needs

'the management process responsible for identifying and satisfying customer needs profitably'
Chartered Institute of Marketing

Selling products that don't come back to people who do

Satisfaction of customer needs at a profit

Dear Mr Manager

I am your customer. When I criticize your food or service – which I will certainly do whenever I am displeased and to anyone who will listen to me – take heed. I am not dreaming up displeasure – the source of it lies in something you have failed to do to make my eating experience as enjoyable as I had anticipated. You must find that source and eliminate it or you will lose me – and my friends as well.

I insist on the right to dine leisurely or eat in haste according to my mood, schedule or other circumstances. I refuse to be rushed and I abhor waiting. This is an important privilege that my money buys from you. And if I am not spending big money with you this particular time, just remember that if you treat me right I will be back later with a larger appetite and more money to spend – and probably with a number of my friends.

I am much more sophisticated these days than I was a few years ago. I've grown accustomed to better things, and my needs are more complex. I'm perfectly willing to spend more money with you – and I have more money to spend – but I insist on quality to match your prices.

Ignore my wants and I will simply cease to exist. Satisfy those wants and I will become increasingly loyal. Add to this satisfaction any little extra personal attention and friendly touches you can dream up – and I will become a walking advertisement for your restaurant.

I am, above all, a human being. I'm sensitive –

especially when I am spending money. I can't stand being snubbed, ignored or looked down upon. I'm proud. My ego needs the nourishment of a friendly personal greeting from you. It is important that you recognize my importance to you – that you appreciate my custom.

Of course, I'm a bit of a show-off too, but don't condemn me for that because you are probably a little hammy at times yourself. Just smile and indulge my whims as best as you can. Remember that while you are feeding me in the literal sense my money is figuratively feeding you.

I am your customer now, but you must prove to me again and again that I have made a wise choice in selecting your restaurant over others. And you must also convince me repeatedly that being a restaurant customer is a desirable thing in the first place. I can, after all, eat at home. But you must provide something extra in food and service – something superior enough to beckon me away from my own table and draw me to yours. You must provide the incentive for me to eat out.

Do we understand each other?

Yours sincerely

The Customer

The Customer

'The business of business is to stay in business.'

The Epicurean siren call to budding restaurateurs is heard by many and occasionally answered by battle-hardened chefs, ambitious waiters or foolhardy idealists.

Nigel was a veteran of city lunches and gourmet dinners who lost no time in purchasing a restaurant in East Sussex when he was offered early retirement.

Within three months the restyled restaurant boasted a 'named chef', obsequious service and obscenely priced wines, mirroring the expense-account lifestyle Nigel had been so familiar with.

Friends and family flattered and fawned faint praise on the opening night, after which their demanding social diaries precluded further visits, when they might have to pay.

Eighteen months later the restaurant foundered on the rocks of reality.

Nigel nursed a cognac and mused over his misfortunes with me late one evening, 'If I'd known what I was letting myself in for I'd never have started. There was hardly a restaurant of note in London I had not eaten in, when I worked in the city, and they all looked so simple to operate.'

Ignorance of the industry and failure to appreciate its somewhat intricate nuances account for untold casualties of new entrants. Just seeing the business solely from the customer's side, without understanding what makes it 'tick', has been the downfall of many aspiring licensees, restaurateurs, guesthouse proprietors and hotel owners.

The Nature of the UK Hospitality Industry

The UK hospitality industry is a diverse mix of large-, medium-, small- and micro-sized enterprises, scattered across the country.

It is estimated that 96 per cent of the hospitality industry is made up of micro (employing up to nine people) and small (employing up to 99 people) businesses. These account for 75 per cent of all employees in an industry which, like the allied areas of leisure and tourism, is dominated by a service ethos.

The high proportion of micro and small businesses is due to:

o Ease of entry into the industry

o Relatively little capital investment required compared with other industries

o No regulatory trade or professional body to oversee or monitor the activities of hospitality enterprises, most of which do not belong to any form of association

o No qualifications necessary as a prerequisite to operate in the industry

How is the Hospitality Industry Distinguished from Leisure and Tourism?

It is difficult to draw a dividing line between hospitality, tourism and leisure. So closely entwined are the activities that they merge with one another. Lundberg (1990) defines a tourist as a visitor who travels at least 100 miles and stays over for at least one night at the destination, as compared with people who travel to a site and return home on the same day. These day-trippers he calls, using American terminology, excursionists.

Consider a package holiday. Which sector does it fit into? Hospitality, leisure or tourism? The holiday involves air travel, during which food and drink will be served. On arrival at the holiday destination, accommodation will be provided at the hotel, where food will be available in a restaurant and drink at the bar.

Leisure facilities at the hotel may include a swimming pool, an exercise gym, a jogging track, or gardens to stroll in. Excursions to tempt holidaymakers (hitherto known as travellers but now metamorphosized into tourists), towards the cultural attractions and local sights abound.

This pot pourri of activities makes it extremely difficult to determine which of the three disciplines is the dominant partner, an uncertainty which complicates the compilation of statistical data. Most tourism and leisure concerns have food and drink at the heart of their provision or as a necessary appendage to their main purpose. Together these hitherto undervalued service industries have become massive sources of revenue for governments world-wide.

The once recognizable trends of a move away from an economy based on manufacturing industry to one that is more and more reliant on services has been reflected in two key indices: employment and tourism spending.

The UK hospitality industry has experienced continual annual growth in employment opportunities and the billions of pounds spent on tourism takes no account of supporting industries who benefit, e.g. kitchen equipment manufacturers, suppliers of furniture, food, drink, crockery etc.

UK Hospitality Characterized by Sector

Although the hospitality industry is an extremely diverse one, it falls naturally into two sectors: commercial and welfare. What distinguishes the two is the focus on the relationship with the customer.

Commercial Sector

In the commercial sector the customer exercises freedom of choice in deciding which hotel, café, restaurant, bar or club to use. Choosing can be confusing given the plethora of 'independent' guidebooks.

Well-known guidebooks for hotels in Britain include *RAC Inspected Hotels: Great Britain and Ireland*, the *Which Hotel Guide*

2000, Recommended Country Houses and Small Hotels: Great Britain and Ireland, Recommended Hotels: Great Britain and Ireland, The Hotel Guide 2000, Best Loved Hotels: England, Wales, Scotland and Ireland and the *Good Hotel Guide*.

These titles are just a few of the publications available, each eager to assert its credentials as *the* authoritative guide to commercial hospitality enterprises.

Some guides carry fiercely independent reviews of hotels; others shamelessly reprint copy supplied to them by the hotel itself, while still others charge for the assessment and subsequent entry.

It is small wonder that many discerning customers at home, not to mention overseas, find it difficult to make an informed choice of which hotel, restaurant, pub or club to visit, when independence and impartiality seldom go hand-in-hand.

The following list for 1999, shows the size and diverse nature of the commercial sector:

Hotels	60,949
Restaurants	15,954
Fast food	2,221
Cafes/takeaways	29,270
Pubs	54,723
Travel	1,359
Leisure	48,523
TOTAL	212,999

Source: *Foodservice Intelligence*

Welfare Sector

In this sector the customer is usually part of a captive audience and the element of choice is removed as in the case of an NHS Trust hospital, a prison, a nursing home, a school or the armed forces.

The figures for this sector in 1997 are shown below.

Staff Catering	20,683
Health Care	25,075
Education	34,429
Services/Welfare	3,355
TOTAL	83,540

Source: *Foodservice Intelligence*

These two sectors can be classified further. The commercial sector is made up of hospitality enterprises that are profit driven, whereas operators in the welfare sector are characterized by cost-recovery principles. Each sector leads to a different emphasis of approach to the marketing function. The commercial sector applies considerable effort to the creative side of marketing but in the welfare sector the emphasis is on the level of quality of delivery of the product and on budgetary control.

Types of Organizations

Product-orientated

These types of organizations develop a product, then throw open their doors and expect the world to beat a path to them to buy it.

They are more interested in selling today's products than in creating new ones to meet customers' changing needs. Such short-sightedness, or marketing myopia, has been the ruination of many businesses who have been unable to see the emergence of competition from other industries. Many engineering companies, for instance, suffered at the hands of plastics manufacturers during the 1960s because they were unable, or unwilling, to address the impact of that new technology.

Sales-oriented

Other organizations may be viewed as 'sales-orientated' i.e. a product is developed and the sales staff promote the product at all costs. The pop music business epitomizes this approach. Most record, tape and CD releases have a limited shelf-life, an average of approximately eight weeks in the charts, during which time as many as possible need to be sold.

Marketing-oriented

A business which is 'marketing-orientated' is one where everybody in the business is concerned with satisfying the customers' wants and requirements to the profit of the business and to the mutual satisfaction of all concerned.

In a marketing-orientated culture, the needs of customers are central to all the key functional disciplines which contribute to running the business (see Figure 1.1). As the minute hand of customers sweeps through the various functions, the hour hand of marketing takes a measured account of their function and impact.

Figure 1.1 The functional disciplines of managing a hospitality enterprise

Some observers feel that the undue emphasis on the profit motive is at the expense of other factors in society; for example:

o The costs to the environment in the provision and manufacture of goods and services is borne by all and not just the immediate consumers. The apparent reluctance of some hospitality operators to promote a healthier lifestyle through their menu choices fails to reflect public concern over dietary issues, such as cholesterol intake, fibre content, etc.

o The physically disabled, who are unable to gain access to some hospitality enterprises, due to the structure and layout of the premises, are discriminated against, albeit inadvertently.

o The inhalation of tobacco smoke by non-smoking guests and members of staff may adversely affect their health.

o The expansion of hospitality operations in suburban areas, resulting in increased environmental noise and nuisance to residents in the locality. The development of new operations in green or brown field sites, destroying landscapes and the country, for subsequent generations.

The counter arguments are powerful in economic terms. The creation of new jobs regenerates local economies and stimulates employment opportunities among a network of supporting infrastructures and suppliers, essential to maintain a business enterprise.

Nevertheless, it is worth remembering that we do not own the environment; we borrow it from our children.

The Marketing Concept

The marketing concept consists of three interdependent propositions:

1. Customer orientation should be the focal point for company decision-making.

2. Such decision-making should produce profitable sales.

3. The entire organization should be aware of customers' needs and wants and work together to meet them.

According to Francis Buttle, when an organization has implemented all three factors, it can then be said to be marketing-orientated.

Purpose of Marketing

The purpose of marketing is to recognise that customers are of critical importance to an enterprise and that profit and the long-term survival of an enterprise depends upon continuing to satisfy customer needs.

Marketing Activities

o The recognition and anticipation of demand

o The stimulation of demand

o The satisfaction of demand

Adopting a marketing philosophy is to put a great deal of effort into 'finding out' about the customer. Such knowledge and understanding influences decisions at every point of the marketing process. The philosophy is represented by the model of marketing in Figure 1.2.

This model shows the importance of discovering and responding to customers' needs: a continual process. Customers' needs change. Yesterday's needs may not be tomorrow's. A marketing-orientated company organizes its resources to anticipate customers' needs and keep in front of the competition to maintain a competitive edge.

The majority of today's customers have increasingly higher expectations and tend to be:

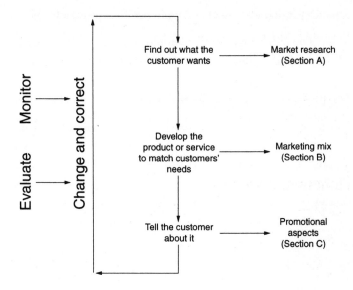

Figure 1.2 A model of marketing

o informed

o confident

o independent

o educated

o consumer-driven

o not bound by traditional demographics

The Office of National Statistics report, *Social Focus on Older People* estimates that advances in health care, increased wealth, and a falling birth-rate mean that 40 per cent of the population will be over 50 years of age and some 20 per cent will be over 80 by the year 2021. The 'Sun, Sea, Saga' generation of those over 50 has tripled this century from 5.6 million in 1901 to 18.8 million in the late 1990s. The report paints a portrait of a new, confident and affluent grey generation who choose to live independent lives and take more foreign holidays each year than their children.

Marketing Hospitality Enterprises

The major difference in marketing hospitality enterprises as against marketing other consumer products is that there is no tangible evidence of the business transaction, compared with the purchase of a material product for example. After a customer has spent money on a meal, a room or a drink, there is nothing to show for it as there is following the purchase of a fridge, microwave oven or compact disc player.

Effective marketing and dynamic selling are more important in the hospitality industry because if a seat in a restaurant or a room in a hotel remains unsold that day, that income is lost forever. This is why many consider the most perishable item in a hotel to be a bedroom. By contrast, in the case of selling consumer products, if a product is not sold today, it might be sold tomorrow.

Summary

o It is often difficult to distinguish between hospitality, leisure and tourism.

o The hospitality industry is dominated by small businesses in the commercial sector.

o Organizations tend to be classified as either product-, sales- or marketing-orientated, but hospitality operators are more marketing-orientated.

o The marketing philosophy is aimed at finding out about customers.

o Customers have no tangible evidence of their purchases.

Finding Out What the Customer Wants

MARKET RESEARCH:
CUSTOMERS

If you don't ask you'll never know.

You won't believe this but there are some hoteliers who just won't listen.

Derek managed a 60-bed suburban hotel in Warwick-shire and prided himself on his social skills with customers, finding out what they felt about the hotel.

'I do my own research – spending hours listening to them all the time'.

Unfortunately he only listened to his regular customers who took advantage of his 'Have-this-one-on-me' routine by telling him what they felt he deserved to hear. This reassured Derek that he was meeting his customers' needs.

Other customers' comments and complaints to staff went unheeded until the hotel proprietor's concern at deteriorating sales prompted action. Derek was last heard of searching for a new job.

Market research is an objective, fact-finding exercise, designed to provide market intelligence in the key areas often known as the three Cs: customers, competitors and costs.

Such research can be either primary or secondary.

Primary Research

Also referred to as field research, this generates information that either does not exist in published form, or is undertaken through use of a questionnaire. There are two categories of primary research:

Quantitative

This deals with factual, quantifiable information:

How old are you?

What type of cuisine do you enjoy the most?

When did you last stay at our hotel?

What type of wine do you prefer?

Qualitative

This probes aspects of customer 'behaviour' which are difficult to quantify, such as their attitudes, opinions and beliefs:

How do you feel about our new cocktail bar?

Relaxed _____ ill at ease

The answers at either end of the scale are the extremes and customers may place themselves anywhere along the line, according to their feeling on the matter.

Exploring customers' subjective reactions is important in the research strategy in order to use the information to influence their behaviour. The area is so critical that it has become a significant branch of marketing studies, known as Consumer Behaviour.

Secondary Research

This uses existing information, e.g. guest history files, previous occupancy rates, or uses external sources of information, e.g. newspaper articles, material from a library, CD ROMs, websites, etc.

Market Research and Marketing Research

Market research describes the location and size of markets, whereas marketing research is much broader and includes discovering customers' views and opinions, collecting objective data from creditable sources, and assessing the results of such investigations.

Market Research Procedure

The most effective research conforms to the following procedure:

1. *Defines the aim of the research accurately*
   An ill-defined, vague or wrongly stated aim leads eventually to valueless results, but their uselessness only becomes apparent after the lengthy research procedure has been completed.

2. *Decides what the objectives are*
   Objectives are the various activities or stages that need to be undertaken in order to achieve the aim of the research. They are much easier to decide upon if the aim has been stated precisely.

3. *Decides upon the most appropriate method(s) to collect the necessary information.*
   This stage involves deciding the most appropriate methods of obtaining the information, the number of people to be surveyed (the sample size), their location and the time allocated to complete this stage.

Collecting information

This is probably the most demanding stage of research in terms of time and effort, for it relies on various methods to collect the required information. Surveys are usually undertaken through a questionnaire conducted on the telephone or by e-mail, or through direct mail, or face to face. All have advantages and disadvantages.

Telephone surveys are used mostly to assess reactions to experiences, and tend to focus on the promotional aspects of marketing. *E-mail surveys* are becoming a potent means of eliciting answers from targeted respondents, because e-mail users have become 'conditioned', in behavioural terms, to respond to information/instructions on a screen. *Direct mail surveys* have long suffered from low reply rates, even with inducements to generate replies, for example discount vouchers. *Face-to-face interviews* are time-consuming but tend to produce more accurate replies than any other kind of survey. There is, however, sufficient anecdotal evidence to suggest that people try to avoid being confronted by researchers conducting face-to-face interviews.

Another method of collecting information on attitudes, feelings and opinions is through a *focus group*. People with similar psychological or demographic characteristics are assembled to discuss an issue chosen by the researchers. Focus groups can provide valuable insights into their attitudes, feelings and opinions, and are often used to test out consumer products, future advertising and promotional campaigns.

How many people should be surveyed?

The question of how many people should be surveyed in order to obtain a meaningful result usually receives the response: 'the sample size must be representative of the whole'! The larger the sample the more reliable the results. However, hospitality operators need not be overly concerned with surveying large numbers of people, for in fact much useful information can be gained from a sample of fewer than 100. According to Kotler

(1997), 'in motivation research studies, fewer than 30 in-depth interviews usually suffice to uncover significant attitudes'.

Sampling methods

The principle methods are as follows:

Simple random sampling. This is not unlike the Lottery – every number (or individual) has an equal chance of being selected.

Stratified random sampling. As the name suggests, this is where the population is divided into strata according to age, income, gender, socio-economic group, or other strata chosen by the interviewer, and a random sample is taken from each stratum.

Cluster sampling. A commonly used approach in which interviewers are directed to find a certain number of interviewees of a particular category, e.g. ten females aged between 21 and 30.

Convenient sample. A group of the most accessible people to hand. This approach may be suitable for a vox pop view but is less satisfactory for most research purposes.

Judgement sampling. Interviewees are selected by the interviewer on the basis of his/her judgement.

Analysing the information

The information provided by a survey may be expressed in various ways: as percentages, in diagrams, pie charts or histograms. This makes it easy to digest at a glance. Most personal computers have excellent software programmes to make the transformation process very easy.

The purpose of any analysis is to provide meaning, and while market research firms cross-reference the information, measure correlation co-efficients, utilize regression analysis and perform goodness of fit tests, most hospitality operators engaging in research will not need to go to these lengths.

Interpreting the findings

The reliability and validity of market rersearch enables the hospitality operator to make judgements and decisions with confidence.

Market Research: Customers

Although an excellent product or service may be offered to the public, one key to success or failure in business is to determine whether there are enough customers willing to buy, on a regular basis and at a price which gives an adequate margin of profit to allow not only for survival of the business but also for further development of the business.

Understanding customers' needs and wants is to determine whether, and how, their needs are being satisfied – where and at what price and under what conditions; what influences their buying decisions; even whether it is profitable to attempt to satisfy them.

To discover whether a market truly exists, it is essential to ask the right questions.

1. How many *potential* customers are there?

2. How many *real* customers are there?

3. Who are they?

4. Who does the buying?

5. Where is the buying done?

6. Where are the customers?

7. What kind of product or service do they want to buy?

8. Why do they want the product or service?

9. Where do they get it at present?

10. How much do they want to pay?

11. What deficiencies are there in the current products or services?

12. When do customers buy, how much and how frequently?

13. Can you deliver what they want, when they want it?

14. Who else can supply this product/service?

15. How strong is the competition?

16. Will the market grow or contract?

Segmenting the market

Since the term 'customers' is so all-embracing, it is necessary to consider buyers (both existing and potential) in various categories or 'segments' of the market. Segmentation of the market gives a better understanding of it and enables a business to increase the effectiveness of its marketing effort.

The particular needs of a discrete segment can be discovered through the use of a questionnaire with a sample of customers, from which conclusions can be drawn. The principle underlying the use of a sample is based on the law of probability familiar to scientists: if the sample is indicative of the total population, then the results will apply to the same.

Market Research Questionnaires

A questionnaire is a list of relevant questions designed to discover views and opinions. Often seen as an art form, there are some important guidelines to consider when designing a questionnaire. Figure 2.1 lists the principal types of questions.

Designing a market research questionnaire

The following are some points to bear in mind:

1. You must be able to make sense of the answers easily, so try to seek answers which are as *specific* as possible. 'Closed questions' are a way of doing this. A closed question provides people with a *limited number* of answers: 'Do you come here once a week/twice a week/more than twice a week?' Instead of 'How often do you come here?' 'Open' questions, where no specific response is suggested, can be useful in soliciting a range of ideas, but they are more difficult to analyse.

2. Think about the *order* of the questions. Don't jump about from one thing to the other – try to establish a logical progression.

3. Work out a way of *excluding people you're not interested in*. For example, if you were opening a wine bar your first question would establish whether the respondent drank wine. (But, in this instance, remember a high proportion of wine bars might be visited by drinkers other than wine lovers.)

4. Ask questions about people's *existing patterns of behaviour*, not about hypothetical ones. For example, 'Do you use e-mail?' rather than 'Would you use e-mail?'

TYPE	EXAMPLE
Dichotomous Offer a yes/no answer.	*Did you book your weekend through our central reservations department?* ☐ *YES*　　　　☐ *NO*
Multiple Offers three or more choices.	*What made you choose our hotel?* ☐ *location*　　☐ *price*　　☐ *reputation* ☐ *accept pets*　　☐ *facilities* ☐ *other (please state)* ....
Likert scale A statement with which the respondent shows the degree of agreement/ disagreement.	*I would warmly recommend this hotel to others.* ☐　　☐　　☐　　☐　　☐ *strongly disagree*　*disagree*　*neither agree nor disagree*　*agree*　*strongly agree*
Semantic differential A scale is inscribed between two bipolar words, and the respondent selects the point that represents their feelings.	*The attitude of the staff is:* *Warm* _____ *Cold* *Attentive* _____ *Disinterested* *Fussy* _____ *Discrete* *Considerate* _____ *Ignorant*
Importance scale A scale that rates the importance of an attribute from 'not at all important' to 'extremely important'.	*We make a point of caring for your pets. Is this:* *extremely important*　*very important*　*somewhat important*　*not very important*　*not at all important* 1 _　　2 _　　3 _　　4 _　　5 _
Rating scale A scale that rates an attribute from 'poor' to 'excellent'.	*How did you rate the selection of wines?* *excellent*　*very good*　*good*　*fair*　*poor* 1 _　　2 _　　3 _　　4 _　　5 _
Completely unstructured A question that respondents can answer in an almost unlimited number of ways. Analysis of such questions can be problematic but the answers can be quite illuminating.	*What do you think of our hotel?*

Figure 2.1 Types of questions

5. In establishing *frequency of use or purchase*, ask 'when' rather than 'how often'. For example: 'When did you last stay in a hotel?' rather than 'How often do you stay in a hotel?'

6. *Avoid ambiguous terms* like 'normally' or 'on average'. People interpret them differently and they don't provide the specific information you need.

7. If you provide categories for answers, make sure *the categories don't overlap*. For instance, if you want information on age, use '18–25; 26–40', not '18–25; 25–40'.

8. *Don't include unnecessary questions.* Personal details, such as respondents' names, may discourage them from answering any questions.

9. *Pilot a draft questionnaire* on a few people before using it, so that any problems can be ironed out and revisions made.

10. Testing people's boredom threshold levels can be avoided by limiting the number of questions asked to about eight. The universal use of questionnaires by all manner of organizations has made questionnaire fatigue an issue to be considered. Variations on a theme to encourage the completion of questionnaires have spurred designers to greater heights in generating maximum responses with minimal effort. The example in Figure 2.2 illustrates what can be achieved with a little imagination.

How satisfied are you?

In our efforts to monitor and improve the food service in the staff restaurant your views would be greatly appreciated.

Please answer the following questions below by placing a tick under "No", "OK", or "Yes" column and include any comments that you would like to make.

	☹️ No	😐 OK	☺️ Yes
Are you served as quickly as you would like?			
Is there a good choice of dishes on offer? *Hot* *Cold*			
Is there a good choice of sweets on offer?			
Are there enough snacks on offer?			
Is there sufficient amount of food served to you?			
Are the hot dishes served hot?			
Is the food well presented?			
Does the food taste freshly cooked?			
Are you satisfied with the cleanliness of the seating area?			
Would you recommend the staff restaurant to your colleagues?			

Please add further comments overleaf

Figure 2.2 A well-designed questionnaire

Some dangers of inadequately designed research

o *Poor questionnaire design* may result in inadequate answers
The respondent may be confused and irritated so that
the answers are not the intended ones.
The respondent may only give you the answer you want
to hear (a particular danger with verbal responses).

o Incorrect lead-in can result in biased answers
If the way a question is put appears to invite criticism,
it will get criticism, even if the respondent would not
normally respond critically.

o Poor selection of respondents can give distorted results
The danger lies in picking those most likely to express
an opinion.

o Inadequate sample size may give misleading results
The sample may be too small to be truly representative.

o Prompting may result in distorted answers
In face-to-face interviews, the interviewer's involvement
in the topic of the research can easily lead to
unconscious prompting. Even a slight change in tone of
voice can achieve this.

Some possible pitfalls in interpreting research findings

o Reading too much into isolated answers.
   One or two strongly expressed answers can often make
   a deep impression, but do the respondents represent
   more than a minority? Even if 10 out of 50 stress that
   they found the food cold, the other 40 may not think
   that, or may have no strong opinion. The 20 per cent
   may be important, but they are not representative.

o Ignoring difficult answers.
   A less than straightforward, or an unexpected answer
   may be ignored but it is always worth investigating as it
   may indicate some aspect not yet perceived. One line of
   research tends to lead to another.

o Finding confirmation of one's opinion.
   It is natural to enjoy feeling right, but it is usually
   critical answers which provide the most scope for
   development.

Research Based on Observation

Observation – the planned and methodical observance of people's
behaviour – is perhaps the simplest form of market research. Lord
Forte used this method to good effect when deciding whether
to buy a milk bar in Oxford Street or Regent Street. He decided
on the one in Regent Street because 'more hungry mouths passed
by it'. From a simple count of pedestrians, Charles Forte's decision
led to a catering enterprise that dominated the UK from the
1970s until its takeover by the Granada Group in 1998.

However, to be effective, such observation needs to be planned
and methodical. It is as well to remember, also, that the results
may not be as valid as those produced by more formal research
methods.

Guidelines for effective observation

o There should be a limited and specific objective to each exercise. It is not practical to try 'general' observation.

o Write down exactly what the problem is that needs clarifying by watching what people do or how they react to certain things.

o Use a series of short observations rather than trying to observe through a long session. This way there will be no loss of concentration; observation will be high of a mixed sample of people.

o Be unobtrusive; do not let people be aware that they are being watched. If observing staff it is as well to warn them beforehand to avoid an attitude of 'snooping'.

o Make notes rather than relying on memory, but remember that 'impressions' are sometimes as important as facts. They can be checked out later by other research methods.

o Summarize findings at the end of each session. Any delay may result in forgetfulness or a tendency to distort findings.

Summary

Both primary and secondary forms of research are an aid to management in order to reduce the risk element in arriving at a decision. In much the same way as military intelligence is an aid to the armed forces, research can:

o give relevant up-to-date information about the market

o indicate trends

o take the guesswork out of decision-making

It cannot:

o provide a miracle cure for a business

o take decisions on behalf of the business

A great deal of emphasis is placed on dicovering and meeting customers' needs. Time spent on this, in an increasingly competitive industry which relies on attracting and maintaining customers, is time well spent.

The fact that there is competition confirms the existence of a market.

Management by walking around (MBWA) is a well-practised method of finding out what's going on in a hotel. Managers cannot manage continually sat behind a desk. The adage 'Off your butt and on your feet, out of the office and into the heat', has been taken to heart by some of the industry's more astute managers.

These people don't confine themselves to their own operation; they make time to visit competitors.

Angela managed a 90-bed hotel in the East Midlands and after seeing a tribute band's performance attract keen interest at a competitor's hotel, decided to do some research into this.

Six months later her hotel's Saturday night cabaret dinners (featuring tribute bands) and overnight accommodation package were so successful that advance bookings were needed.

The Competition

Types of competition

The first step is to identify what constitutes the competition. There are two types of competition: direct and indirect.

Direct competition is between businesses that offer the same or similar products or types of services. Two pub restaurants, opposite one another, offering a similar range of products (beers, wines and menu items) would be in direct competition for customers.

Indirect competition is between business organizations competing for the same discretionary income of customers. For example, customers may choose to spend an evening drinking socially in a wine bar or a pub, or go for an Italian or Chinese meal, or visit the theatre, go to the cinema, visit a bowling alley, or stay at home and watch television!

The variety of opportunities available to spend their time and money illustrates the intense nature of a competitive environment.

Where is the competition?

After identifying both direct and indirect competitors, the next step is to identify where they are based within the catchment area from which the business draws its custom.

A catchment area is the geographical area where existing and potential customers live and/or work. It may be expressed in terms of distance and/or time, i.e. how much time customers are prepared to take travelling to the location of the restaurant, bar, hotel, club, etc.

The catchment area for the hotel shown in Figure 3.1 would include potential customers from the following locations:

The *housing area* provides customers to drink in the bars or eat in the restaurant. There may be various clubs and societies in the area that need a meeting venue – a function room in the hotel could satisfy that need.

Bus terminus and railway station. Passengers may be a mix of day trippers and commuters working in the shops, offices and industrial estate, who may choose to use the bars, coffee shop or restaurant of the hotel.

The *industrial estate* will attract visitors, and also firms' representatives, some of whom will require overnight accommodation and may use the hotel restaurant to entertain clients.

The infrastructure of a market town is considerably more intricate than Figure 3.1 suggests, but the example shows how establishing accurately from where custom is drawn adds considerably to the bank of intelligence a hospitality enterprise must build up.

Time has been mentioned as the other factor that determines a catchment area. There is much empirical evidence to suggest that customers looking to celebrate an occasion are not inclined to visit a local hotel or restaurant for a meal – 'It's too near home'! An occasion merits a car journey of about thirty minutes from

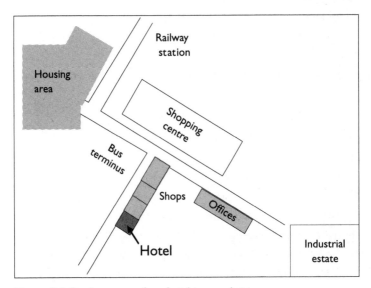

Figure 3.1 Catchment area for a hotel in a market town

their home. The combination of the journey and the event appear to enhance the sense of celebration. There is a perverse logic that suggests the longer the journey, the more significant the celebration. This has been held to be true even when a Michelin-starred restaurant is situated only a mile from home.

How much do competitors charge?

To produce something better a business needs to know competitors' prices and what they include. The service or product to be supplied must either be of a better quality or at a cheaper price. There must be a good reason why customers should move their custom.

Assessing the competition involves answering the following questions:

o How many hospitality enterprises are in direct competition?

o What facilities do they offer (e.g. restaurant, function rooms, coffee shop)?

o What is unique about them?

o What is the quality of these facilities?

o What prices do they charge?

o Are there any noticeable gaps in the facilities, quality or value for money on offer?

If there is no competition it is worth asking why. Could it be that there is not enough demand to justify a supplier? It could be a case of nobody having considered the idea of supplying, or it could be that they have tried and failed. Talking to suppliers and networking with colleagues and operators in the locality can often provide missing pieces of the jigsaw to complete the picture.

Consider the following little homily which is a poignant, back-handed compliment to competitors:

My competitors do more for me than my friends do.
My friends are too polite to point out my weaknesses,
but my competitors go to great expense to advertise them.

My competitors are efficient, intelligent and attentive;
they force me to search for ways to improve my service.

My competitors would take my customers away from me
if they could. This keeps me alert to hold what I have.
If I have no competitors I might become complacent and
inattentive. I need the discipline which they force upon me.
I salute my competitors, they have been good to me.
God bless them all.

Costs

The costs incurred in starting up a new business are governed by the business's location.

City centre, suburban or rural: a location in any one of these areas will be reflected in the price of the land, lease, local authority charges and insurance premiums.

The style of operation determines the cost of labour employed. Typically a prestigious hotel might aim for a labour cost of around 40 per cent of sales, whereas a fast food operation aims for 12 per cent.

Cost of finance (e.g. bank loan), rent, depreciation, overheads, all have to be allowed for before realizing a net profit.

Minimizing the cost of materials without sacrificing quality, keeping a tight rein on the cost of labour and controlling overheads are all aimed at maximizing profit. This is akin to walking a tight-rope, trying to balance what it costs to produce a service against what customers are prepared to pay, i.e. what the market will bear.

The market research on costs concentrates on secondary sources of information since most of it will necessarily be factual and precise.

Benefits of market research

- Helps to define a place in the existing market.

- Reveals opportunities for variation in the range of products or services offered.

- Reveals opportunities for variation in the quality of products or services offered.

- Reveals opportunities for the type or extent of customer service offered.

- Provides information regarding future trends in demand.

- Provides an evaluation of advertising and promotional methods.

- Reveals opportunities for better and more effective advertising and promotion.

Summary

Market research is:

- knowing who the present customers are;

- investigating potential customers and analysing their needs;

- deciding which customers the business will satisfy;

- assessing the product and how far it meets the needs of existing and potential markets;

- assessing competitors and the facilities they offer;

- taking into account national/local changes and trends; and

- relating the results of investigation to the return on investment.

In conclusion, it is important to realise that long-term profitability relies on *continued* satisfaction for the customer. Care must be taken, therefore, to assess the product not only in terms of increased *profitability*, but also in terms of *value to the customer*. In this connection, it is often more realistic to cater for customers with similar tastes for product and atmosphere. Too many differing interests can have an adverse effect on customer satisfaction, which competitors may quickly exploit by appealing to their needs more accurately.

'My market is split between the "haves" and "have nots"; those who "have not" eaten here are my potential target market',

SAID MIKE, A BULL-NOSED, RAUCOUS RESTAURANT MANAGER WITH A PENCHANT FOR UNDERSTATEMENTS.

'The market' is not a single entity where all buyers' needs are the same and all products aimed at meeting those needs are identical. Market segmentation is the division of a large market into a number of smaller segments. It is a process of dividing the market into buyer groups with different needs.

Targeting the Market

The hospitality industry is faced with a heterogeneous market, i.e. customers who are seeking differently priced accommodation, according to their budget; different meal experiences, from self-service to silver service; different styles of cuisine, from Creole to Thai; alternative take-away meals, from burgers to sandwiches.

The strategies available to hospitality operators fall into three areas:

1. *Undifferentiated marketing*: trying to attract as many people as possible to buy – also referred to as mass marketing. The focus in on what is common, as opposed to what is different, and on producing a product that has a broad appeal, e.g. hot dog from a mobile vendor.

2. *Differentiated marketing*: trying to appeal to a variety of different groups. Hotels are prime examples of differentiated marketing with their variety of 'products' and market segments. A function room is a single 'product' but is sold for many different purposes: interview room, sales meeting, social gathering, celebratory event, etc. Supplement that function room with other products, e.g. morning coffee, afternoon tea, buffet lunch, fork buffet lunch (with or without wine and non-alcoholic refreshments), and the differentiated marketing permutations become almost infinite. The aim is to differentiate clearly customers into homogenous groups in order to direct products tailored to appeal to that discrete segment of the market.

3. *Niche marketing*: concentrating on a particular segment of the market. By concentrating on one segment of the market, a business acquires the specialist knowledge and reputation to be regarded as the market leader. The idea of putting all the eggs in one basket is not without risk if the market segment takes a downward turn, but the rewards tend to be high.

Methods of Segmenting the Market

There are a variety of different ways of segmenting the market, but the more common methods include:

o By specific products and services

o By types of customer group/types of buyer

o By size of customer group

o By geographical location

Market segmentation is market-orientated rather than product-orientated. It is concerned with identifying distinct customer groups. For example, the market for a city centre bar/restaurant could be segmented in various ways:

o **By specific products and services:**
   List of food menu items
   List of alcoholic and non-alcoholic beverages.

o **By customer group/type of buyer**
   Lunch-time city workers
   Lunch-time shoppers
   Early evening city workers
   Late evening socializers

o **By size of customer group**
   Large groups of lunch-time customers to small groups of late evening socializers

o **By geographical location**
   The number of potential customers in each area, classified into say:
   50 yards (lunch-time city workers)
   7 miles (out-of-town shoppers)
   15 miles (late-night socializers)

Each of the four sections above could be sub-divided further.

To be attractive to the business each segment would ideally possess the following features:

1. It would be large enough to justify attention

2. It would have potential for further growth

3. It would be dominated by current competition

4. There would be unsatisfied needs which the business could competently serve

Each factor needs careful consideration and market research would be necessary to ascertain the size, competitiveness and profit potential of particular segments.

The process of segmentation helps to clarify the profile(s) of chosen customer groups. Such clearly defined groups are featured in Figure 4.1, which illustrates the typical family *life-cycle passage*

Bachelor Stage: young single people

Young married couples with no children

Full nest 1: young married couple with children

Full nest 2: older married couples still with dependent children

Empty nest: older married couples with no dependent children

Older single people: still working or retired

Figure 4.1 Family life-cycle

of an individual. These stages in life are typified by predictable patterns of behaviour.

o Bachelor stage: young, single, living away from home with few financial burdens, conscious of style and fashion, recreation-orientated.

o Young married couples with no children – financially better off than they will be in the future. This group has the highest purchase rate of durable items.

o Young married couples with children – home-buying at a peak, net disposable income severely reduced, less influenced by advertising messages.

o Older married couples with dependent children – improved financial position when wives often return to resume their careers, high average purchase of durable items.

o Older married couples with no dependent children – financially more secure, home ownership at a peak, little interest in new products, increased interest in travel and recreation.

o Older single people working or retired – increasingly concerned with their state of health; retirement causes cut in income and purchases tend to be on essential items.

However, for many people such life passages are not the norm. There are substantial numbers of separated and divorced couples and many families are the product of second marriages. These groups are equally discrete segments of the market with their own particular needs.

Having segmented the market, three options present themselves:

1. To ignore the differences in customer needs and develop a product or service which concentrates on the common needs of the potential customers.

2. To recognize the wide range of different customer needs and produce a wide range of products and services, tailored to meet as many of these as possible.

3. To recognize the existence of a wide range of needs of different customer groups, but focus on a narrow range of products and services, aiming for a few chosen groups only.

None of the above basic strategies is necessarily better than the other. The question is, which is most appropriate to a business at a particular stage of its development? However, point 3 is often a useful initial strategy for a new business, provided that there are adequate numbers of customers in a particular chosen segment.

On the other hand, the small business which has recognized customer needs which are not fully being met and is prepared to tailor its products and services accordingly, promote, price and make them available in a slightly different manner, can often carve out a 'niche' in the market in which it can establish itself.

Important though the family cycle is, some operators place greater emphasis on other demographic variables when segmenting the market.

Socio-economic tables have sometimes been seen to be a valuable indicator of the breakdown of the population for marketing purposes, although they are of greater relevance to national hospitality enterprises rather than to the proprietor of a small restaurant.

Although seemingly dated and, in some quarters, politically unacceptable to divide society into social classes, it nevertheless remains a fact that the Royal Mail post code areas display a clustering of individuals belonging to the same social class. This has a bearing on and is a reflection of property prices, which in turn reflect their owners' incomes and their occupations.

Income is closely related to socio-economic grouping. The higher the group the higher the level of income. However the higher groups (A and B) tend to be asset-rich and cash-starved,

Social Grade	Social Status	Occupation	Approximate % of population
A	Upper middle class	Higher managerial and administrative or professional	3
B	Middle class	Middle managerial, administrative or professional	10.9
C1	Lower middle class	Supervisory or clerical, junior managerial	21.7
C2	Skilled working class	Skilled manual workers	32
D	Working class	Semi and unskilled manual workers	23.7
E	Those at the lowest level of subsistence	Pensioners, casual or lowest grade workers, unemployed	8.7

i.e. their levels of disposable income may be akin to groups C and D but their patterns of expenditure will vary according to their lifestyle preferences.

This has important implications for hospitality operators as higher income groups tend to eat out at a higher-than-average spend per head.

Psychographic segmentation has become increasingly important to marketers as traditional lifestyles have been overturned or cast aside by an increasingly independent new generation who have turned away from the old order. Hospitality operators are responding accordingly through an increasing casualization of service in themed restaurant bars, dropping dress codes for hotel restaurants, supplying designer beers and lagers by the neck in bars, ignoring the conventions of serving from the right, take away from the left, and so on.

The characteristics of consumers tends to reflect the types of people they are. Rogers identified five psychological types of people, to which Buttle has added personal and social characteristics in the following table of adaptor categories:

	Personal characteristics	*Social characteristics*
Innovators	Risk-takers, venturesome, like new ideas, cosmopolitan	Socially aggressive, communicative
Early Adopters	Enjoy prestige as competent, knowledgeable early adopters, less venturesome than innovators; respectable, enjoy leadership; tend to reinforce opinion leadership position through seeking objective product information	Socially well-integrated; gregarious; influential of others' buying
Early Majority	Tend to conform to social trends and follow opinions of early adopters; more traditional outlook; upper social classes	Well-integrated socially
Late Majority	Orientated towards local or family events; not responsive to change; sceptical; follow the majority	Less gregarious than early majority
Laggards	Suspicious of change, cautious, conservative, cost-conscious, impervious to social pressure	Socially isolated

Table 4.1 Psychographic segmentation

Society's pace-setters create innovative ideas and styles and taste and are closely allied to early adopters. These two categories lead opinion and exert influence on society at large.

Summary

o Markets can be segmented by demographic or geographic means, or by products and services or size of the customer market.

Develop the Product or Services to Match Customers' Needs

'Forecasting is like trying to drive a car blindfolded following directions given by someone looking out of the back window.'

One of the stock questions at a job interview is 'Where do you expect to be in five years' time?'

The equally stock answer reveals the aims, ambitions, aspirations and expectations of enthusiastic candidates for the vacant post.

The rationale of the question applies equally to every hospitality enterprise.

However, the indices for achieving the planned goal are more rigorous in business. For companies listed on the stock exchange the financial markets deliver their verdict on a company's end of year achievements by reappraising their share price. There can be no better form of objective independent assessment.

Although the majority of hospitality enterprises are small independent organizations, they too need to plan ahead.

Forecasting

Forecasting has never been an easy task as no one can accurately predict the future. Nevertheless, enterprises make every effort to gather and pool data: they take into account trends, assess economic indicators, review historical patterns of business activity in order to amass the best available information upon which forecasted plans are based.

The accuracy of any forecast can be monitored over time and adjustments made to the plan, when required. A plan gives a sense of purpose to activity; it marks out a route from start to finish and shows the direction to take. The mnemonic SMART indicates how to give a plan that disciplined edge.

S Simple (explained in clear unambiguous terms)
M Measurable (so that it can be quantified)
A Achievable (success breeds success)
R Realistic (not over-ambitious nor under-challenging)
T Time-bound (a fixed timescale)

Planning for the future stems from an appraisal of the present, which requires an analysis of current business activity.

To analyse the business is to check out thoroughly that the business is matching customer needs most profitably and provide a base for plans and improvements.

Any method of setting out fact, evidence and information should:

o provide an objective picture of the products and services on offer;

o be constructively critical of the business;

o allow those involved in the business to stand back and see themselves as others see them.

A useful means of appraising the business is the SWOT (Strengths, Weaknesses, Opportunities and Threats) analysis.

Strengths and weaknesses are internal to the business and usually within their control; opportunities and threats are external to the business and generally outside the control of the firm. This approach can be used for any or all of the functions of a hospitality enterprise, i.e. marketing, operations, human resources, finance. The following is an example of a SWOT analysis relating to the marketing of a hotel:

Functional Area	Strengths	Weaknesses
	Strong brand name Location Effective sales team	Limited product range Inflexible pricing policy
Marketing	Opportunities	Threats
	Growth of overseas visitor traffic Link with new heritage centre to promote weekend breaks	New hotel planned to open in 12 months

This method of analysis should be applied to the business as a whole and individual profit centres.

Assumptions and guestimates inevitably have to be made, particularly concerning external factors outside the control of the business, such as interest rates, outbreaks of hostilities, or the impact of new European legislation. The effects of which can wreck even the best-made plans.

Quo vadis?

Too narrow a defnition of what business we are in can result in a myopic view of the market and can exclude opportunities.

This is caused by enterprises thinking purely in terms of what their products offer as opposed to the needs they *might* satisfy. The rhetorical question 'What business are we in?' unshackles constrained thought, and the supplementary question 'What business do we want to be in?' can encourage fertile minds to explore possibilities for survival either by natural organic evolution or radical revolution.

Ansoff's matrix (Figure 5.1) provides a useful means of assessing alternative business strategies.

P R O D U C T S

	Existing	New
Existing	Market penetration	Product development and expansion
New	Market expansion	Diversification (the great unknown)

(vertical label: **M A R K E T S**)

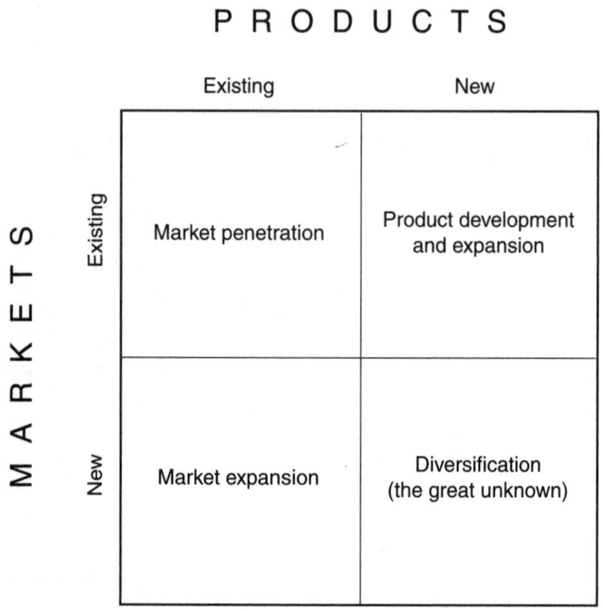

Figure 5.1 Alternative business strategies

In relation to a hotel, Ansoff's matrix may be interpreted thus.

Market penetration: is aimed at increasing the usage of existing products by an existing market to increase market share. In a hotel this could mean seeking more business users for hotel bedrooms mid-week and to achieve higher occupancy rates.

Market expansion: is aimed at seeking new markets for existing products. A hotel might actively target leisure interest groups to promote weekend breaks and increase occupancy rates at the weekend.

Product development and expansion: introducing new products to existing markets, e.g. introducing pay per view videos for hotel residents, a new coffee shop in a hotel, a new range of cocktails.

Diversification: whereas the other three strategies involve either marketing skills or product technology, or a combination of both, diversification offers a less clearly defined route. This growth sector tends to evolve from either the market expansion or the product development sectors, rarely is the leap made directly from market penetration. For example, one hotelier noted the growth in long-term residential care for the elderly and turned his hotel into a nursing home. This bold step of diversification took the business into a different 'industry' altogether and heralded a new appraisal of the business, using Ansoff's matrix, which brings us back to where we began: by looking at products and markets.

Planning

A customer's decision (to buy or not to buy) is seldom attributable to one reason only. Therefore the business can influence the buying decision in a number of ways. These are generally classified under four headings and are known as the Marketing Mix (or the four Ps).

o Product

o Promotion

o Price

o Place

Some authors speak of five Ps (the fifth being Presentation). Others speak of seven Ps by including People and Positioning. Most agree, however, that there are at least four.

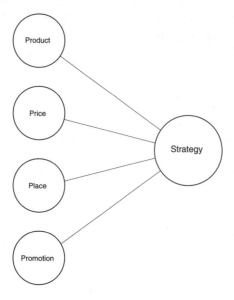

Figure 5.2 The marketing mix

The purpose of the mix is to devise a marketing plan which many regard as a blueprint for designing the future (see Figure 5.2). The marketing function must acquire sufficient understanding of customers' needs to generate a sufficient mix of products, at the right time, with the right level of promotion and at the optimum price.

Summary

o SMART helps forecasting

o SWOT helps assess the future of a business

o Alternative business strategies crystallize options for a business

o The marketing mix of four Ps is used to develop a marketing strategy for the business

'A product is what it does.'

Products

An auto-engineer might describe a product such as a car in terms of its torque, compression ratio, drag co-efficient factor, type of tensile steel used for construction, and so on. Customers do not buy product specifications: the motive for their purchase is what it will do for them.

A marketer would mention the features of the car but stress the benefits according to what the customer's needs might be. If the customer's interest is in fuel consumption then the marketer would refer to the low drag co-efficient which gives more miles per litre.

All manufactured products have features from which benefits are derived and those are what the customer buys.

Hospitality Products

Products do not only satisfy economic, functional and technological needs, they also serve to meet the aesthetic, emotional and psychological needs of customers.

What a product does for one customer may not be what it does for another. The various motives for eating a meal are evidence of that.

What does a meal do? Stave off starvation? Become a means of celebrating a birthday? Serves to impress a business client, or engender team spirit at a sales conference? The reasons why people eat out vary; Wearne (1994) gives the following: convenience, escape, to be with others, a meeting place, a food experience, a special occasion, somewhere casual. Some reasons may be linked to the type of service sought: buffet, carvery, brasserie or silver service.

The choice of a restaurant implies rational choice on the part of the customer, but people are surprisingly fickle and will be influenced by less relevant factors, such as the restaurant's reputation, name, claims to fame, siting and ease of access, entrance, image, colour scheme, degree of illumination, etc.

Ephemeral, subjective and almost wholly immeasurable factors drive market researchers and hospitality operators to pursue a successful formula. Those who have caught the public's imagination have triumphed and replicated the formula through a chain of establishments. But the chains continually adapt their products and services to meet customers' changing tastes.

Products of the Hospitality Industry

Products provided by the hospitality industry in all its various forms are predominantly service-orientated. Stripped down to the bare essentials, hotels are establishments in which to eat, drink, and sleep. Each of these activities relates to what may be termed a 'core product', i.e. restaurant, bar, bedroom.

The fundamental benefit that the customer receives from a hotel is sleep, food, and drink.

The 'product' can be described in various terms:

The *formal product* is the way the core product is translated physically, e.g. the size of the bedroom, the type of menu, the range of drinks.

The *augmented product* is the complete product offering. All hotels offer the same core product but they are modified and enhanced to appeal to target markets through mechanisms such as levels of customer care, price differentials, etc.

The three levels of a product are:

Core product
(e.g. Hotel bedroom)

Formal product
Quality (high levels of comfort), features (king-size beds, personal jacuzzi), styling (aesthetically pleasing), brand name (hotel's reputation), packaging (rooms individually named)

Augmented product
The totality of benefits
(24-hour room service, non-smoking rooms, rooms with panoramic views, personal valet service)

Equally important as the products offered is the service. Some would say that the only 'product' the hospitality industry produces is customer satisfaction. Elements such as accommodation, food and drink are necessary to process the product, without which the final product would be incomplete.

Intangible service elements are a dominant factor within the broad church of the hospitality industry. The following comparisons between a service and a material product serve to emphasize why service is crucial:

Service versus product characteristics

A Service	A Material Product
Provided by humans	Made mostly by machines
Involves customers directly	Independent of customers
Is intangible	Tangible
Cannot be owned, used or stored	Can be owned, used and stored
Standardization of quality is difficult to maintain	Made to a standardized level of quality

The basic characteristics of services identified by Murdick, Render and Russell (1990) show the areas where something can go awry. Because of these potential trouble spots, service management must take a total organizational approach that makes quality of service, as perceived by the customer, the number one driving force for the operation of the hospitality business.

1. Services are intangible output.

2. Services produce variable, non-standard output.

3. A service is perishable. It cannot be carried in inventory, but is consumed when produced.

4. There is considerable customer contact throughout the service process.

5. The customer participates in the provision of service.

6. Skills are sold directly to the customer.

7. Services cannot be mass-produced.

8. Acute personal judgement is employed by individuals performing the service.

9. Service firms are labour-intensive.

10. Decentralization facilities are located near the customers.

11. Measures of effectiveness are subjective.

12. Quality control is primarily limited to process control.

13. Pricing options are elaborate.

Nothing stays the same for ever. Customers' attitudes change; the music they enjoyed listening to ten years ago may not be quite to their taste today. Just as customers' tastes change, so do their needs, with the result that new products are introduced as existing ones become outdated, and eventually obsolete.

This process closely resembles the human life-cycle. The phases of birth, growth, maturity and old age parallel the concept of the *product life-cycle*, which typically moves through four phases: Introduction; Growth; Maturity; Decline (see Figure 6.1).

Introduction
Launching a new product demands time, promotion costs and good management.

Growth
In this phase the product enjoys an exponential rise in demand as it grows from strength to strength until demand levels out, indicating the onset of maturity. Provided the product has proved sufficiently strong enough to overcome the resistance of innovators' established buying habits, then early adopters boost and continue to boost sales as the early majority follows the crowd until a plateau is reached.

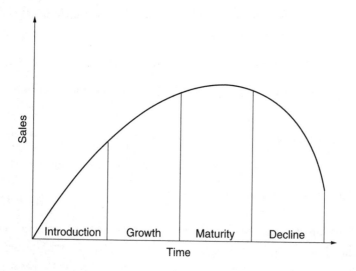

Figure 6.1 Product life-cycle

Maturity

This stage can be extremely long. Some well-known products have been in existence for over 40 years and the initial investment will have been be recouped many times over. Sales growth reduces as sales volume levels out, indicating repeat purchases of the products.

Decline

The change from maturity to old age is often imperceptible to a family, but very clear to outsiders. So it is with products. Marketers have the advantage of being able to monitor changes in demand and can predict the onset of growth maturity and decline. In doing so they can market inputs accordingly.

Inevitably, the loyalty of customers is tested as new products supercede the existing ones, or customers are distracted and tempted by alternatives.

Advances in medical science and the application of cosmetic surgery can do much to mask the effects of time on the human body. Products too can be similarly rejuvenated to prolong their lives. In the case of a hotel, refurbished bedrooms, newly designed menus, discount offers to early-bird diners, are all attempts to prolong the maturity/arrest the decline phase in the product life-cycle.

Eventually, though, a product may owe more to its past than to the future, and when that stage is reached it would be a kindness to replace it.

Summary

o Products are core, formal and augmented

o Services are intangible

o Products go through a life-cycle

o Product life-cycles can be extended

o Time is no respecter of a product's age

The only places with a captive audience are prisons and hospitals, although airlines run them a close second.

Place and Location

The place is where the product is sold and for commercial hospitality enterprises location is often the key to success. When deciding where to build his next hotel Charles Hilton had three considerations and in order of priority they were location, location and location.

Products designed to satisfy known market needs must be made readily available to customers, i.e. at the right place and at the right time.

The marketing aspects which might be classified as referring to place are:

Location

Distribution channels

Geographical coverage

Influences on the physical location of the business relate to:

The number of customers in the catchment area

The presence or otherwise of competitors

The cost

For example, a city centre sandwich bar needs a central location to maximize sales opportunities, which could be further enhanced through a delivery service (distribution channel). However, a restaurant might choose a remote location to enhance its unique status which can act like a magnet to draw in custom from far and wide.

The pressure of competition can be a compelling factor in joining a gastronomic enclave of restaurants offering identical food. The 'China Towns' of London and Manchester, the 'curry mile' in Rusholme, South Manchester and the 'Balti belt' in Sparkbrook, Birmingham epitomize this.

However, products are not always sold exclusively at one location. Hotels sell bedroom accommodation through coach operators, central reservations offices, consortia, tourist boards, travel agents and web sites; these are their channels of distribution, the purpose of which is to widen the opportunity to increase sales revenue.

Distribution Channels

For channels to be effective information from the hospitality operator should flow to customers. The amount of information is decided by the sender, it may take the form of salient points (such as a hotel's location, room rates, special attractions) and be underpinned by promotional literature focusing on those aspects.

Direct channels provide the hospitality operator with maximum control over the distribution of information.

But the use of indirect channels or intermediaries significantly multiplies opportunities for the hospitality enterprise to generate interest and potential income. Jones and Lockwood (1989) identify four types of intermediary.

o Corporate sales offices and central observations of the hotel itself as well as referral sales from other hotels in the chain.

o Organizations whose main business is the promotion and sale of travel and accommodation, such as travel agents, hotel representatives, computerized reservations services, tour operators, and incentive travel planners.

o Organizations who offer travel and accommodation as a complementary service to their main business activity: such as American Express, car rental companies, and motoring organizations.

o Organizations with a general interest in the promotion and organization of tourism, such as tourist boards, tourist information centres and convention and conference bureaux.

However, the growth of information technology and the spread and increasing convenience of personal computers will enlarge the e-commerce market and bring into sharp relief the use of web sites.

Summary

o   Hospitality operations often depend on location for success.

o   The place and positioning of an operation can be improved on by channels of distribution.

o   Channels of distribution are means of increasing sales.

Costs are a matter of fact, price is a matter of policy.

Nobody buys blind, or do they?

Skilled restaurant staff are past masters at persuading customers to buy regardless of price. The scene is a familiar one: a couple quietly dining in the restaurant, contemplating the menu, and mentally noting the prices, while the waiter/waitress brightly tells them of items not appearing on it. In almost a conspiratorial whisper the couple are alerted to wild salmon, lobster, or mussels to start with, temptingly followed by roast pheasant or duck.

It is a brave soul who is not tempted to order 'off menu' and, guess what? No one asks the price or queries the bill.

Price decisions are rarely easy to make and should not be made independently of the other elements of the marketing mix. The product, place, price and promotion strategies must be compatible and mutually supportive.

A market selling products/services which already exist, may well be a mature market. In this case, the products will be associated with well-known going prices, and the pricing decision is clearly less complex than in the case of pricing something entirely new.

In making a pricing decision a hospitality business needs to take into consideration the:

Value of the product or service to the customer

Price as an indicator of quality

Volume of sales forecast by the business

Competitors' offerings

Value of the Product or Service to the Customer

As beauty lies in the eye of the beholder, so value lies in the mind of the customer. Products held in high regard are usually associated with quality – whether it's a leather bag from Mulberry, afternoon tea at the Sharrow Bay Country House Hotel, or lunch at the Savoy Grill.

The relationship between the value or worth of a product and the price charged, reflecting the element of quality, has been represented as follows:

$$\text{Value} = \frac{\text{Quality}}{\text{Price}}$$

Price as an Indicator of Quality

Hospitality operators reverse this statement by putting quality to the fore as an indicator of price. Hotels are rated by the motoring organizations' star system; thus a five-star hotel will be more expensive than a three-star hotel because it offers a higher quality of service, standards and products. Although this perception may be slightly misplaced, as the stars are awarded only on the *facilities* provided by the hotel, customers associate the stars and the tourist board's Crown classification system with quality.

Volume of Sales Forecast by the Business

Sales forecasting has a direct bearing on pricing strategy.

Market research may have identified the price band customers are willing to pay but cost considerations and profit levels need to be taken into account before arriving at a decision. The matrix on pages 68–9 shows the different types of pricing strategy which take a more market-orientated approach.

Pricing decisions are subject to three main factors:

The customer

The competition

The costs

The first two of these are concerned with market influences while the third relates to the type of operation.

The Influence of the Market on Pricing Strategy

Ultimately, the price charged must be one which the market is prepared to pay. Moreover, enough customers are needed to make the whole business profitable.

It is probably safe to say that the higher the price charged in relation to that of the competition, the less will be sold. Often the degree to which price-cutting will help increase sales, is constrained by the ability and willingness of competitors to respond with similar tactics. A low price strategy may appear

Pricing Strategy matrix

Pricing strategy	Objectives
Lower price: market penetration or sales-orientated strategy	Gain entry into new market. Capture customers from competitors. Increase sales volume. Attract customers to sample or test product. Attract repeat business
High price: profit-orientated strategy	Maximization of profit. Rapid payback of investment
Competition-oriented or multi-price strategy	To match competitors' pricing. To obtain share of existing market by comparison selling

Source: Roberts, J., *Marketing for the Hospitality Industry*

Advantages	Disadvantages	Marketing and sales activity
Low price may attract customers to sample a trial product. Differentiates operator's product (if of same type) to competitors' products. Is appropriate in times of inflation or recession	Possible low customer esteem of product (low price means low quality). Starting with low price makes price rises difficult. Larger sales volume needed to return reasonable profits. Slow payback of investment	Selling by price. Need for aggressive sales activities. Need to clearly identify potential demand and profit/costs. Product-orientated selling
High price will equate with high quality worth or value. Easier to reduce price when market circumstances allow or enforce. Some markets are insensitive to a high-price strategy	Risk that high price will not equate with high quality	Selling or quality worth or benefit. Related high costs of promotion and sales
Maintains element of differentiation. Competes at same level with competitors	Possible need to differentiate products in other ways. Differing unit costs may affect real profit margins. Differing units may be in different market positions	Need to sell by comparison. Need to target activity precisely. Marketing will need in the end to differentiate the product from competitors' products

on the surface to be an easy way of breaking into a competitive market but can also be very dangerous!

As with every 'rule' there is always an exception. Price may not be an issue for some customers and there are those who are more than willing to pay for exclusivity, and the hospitality industry is well placed to cater for this tendency.

The Influence of Costs on Pricing Strategy

Though it is the market which will in the end determine the price which can be charged, that price must be paid by sufficient people to cover all costs, and give at least a minimum required profit.

It is therefore important to get the pricing strategy right. Knowledge of the costs of the business and how such costs behave is extremely important.

To survive and prosper a business must recover all its costs before it generates profits, and a hospitality enterprise, like any other, incurs costs even when there are no customers.

Business costs fall into two main categories:

Fixed Costs (Overheads)

These costs are not related directly to the level of business activity but often to the passage of time, e.g. rent for the year, annual insurance premiums, etc. These costs do not vary as the volume of business increases or decreases. They are 'fixed'.

Variable Costs (Direct Costs)

These costs vary directly with the level of business activity, i.e. a doubling of sales will lead to a doubling in total direct costs.

Examples of such variables are:

> raw materials
> cost of goods sold

It is particularly important to know the costs of the product or service on offer so that the necessary contribution to overheads and profit from sales can be established. The concept 'contribution' refers to sales value less direct costs and is a very useful tool for financial planning generally.

The break-even chart (Figure 8.1) illustrates how costs and sales relate to the volume of sales.

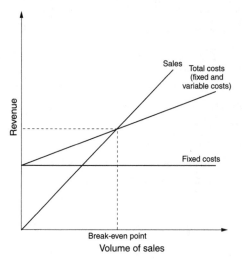

Figure 8.1 Break-even chart

Setting a Price

Buttle categorizes the options available into *profit-orientated, sales-orientated, competitor-orientated,* and *cost-orientated.* Jones and Lockwood are similarly persuaded by this view, and devote several pages to explaining the intricacies of each category.

> The *profit-orientated* approach focuses on a desirable return on the amount of capital invested.
> The *sales-orientated* approach takes into consideration the market, the competition and channels of distribution to produce a variety of prices of the same

product. For example, the price received for a hotel bedroom may be rack rate for a direct sale, discounted if bought on line through the internet, and discounted even further if purchased through a tour operator.

Competitor-orientated pricing takes no account of the financial structure of the business in terms of profit ratios, return on capital, or operating costs. This approach is geared to either matching or undercutting direct competitors' prices and aimed at maintaining or increasing market share.

Cost-orientated pricing is usually based on the cost plus principle of adding a percentage mark-up or a set amount to the cost of the item. The simplicity of this method accounts for its widespread use. It may not always be sensible to adopt this policy, whatever the accounts department might think. A marketing-orientated businesses treat pricing as a marketing decision, not an accounting responsibility.

Summary

o Price is not independent of other elements of the marketing mix

o Costs are either fixed or variable

o Hospitality enterprises have high fixed costs

Tell the Customer All About It

'Getting customers and keeping them are the only aspects of a business which create revenue, all other aspects create costs.'

Harry and Jane were the new tenants of the Roebuck Inn and like most licensees keen to announce their arrival. The tired old statement 'under new management' held no appeal; they felt they could do better, and did. A large banner draped outside the pub said it all: 'They've gone!' Business boomed; apparently the previous tenants were universally loathed.

Hospitality enterprises cannot rest on the laurels of their success and assume that their exisiting clientele will remain loyal for life. Customers may be tempted to switch their allegiance after trying a new competitor, or move to another area. Either way, some existing business is lost and has to be replaced.

Attracting new business brings into sharp focus the means and methods available to promote the enterprise, but regrettably not all effort is matched by reward. 'Some you win, some you lose.' Figure 9.1 demonstrates this fact.

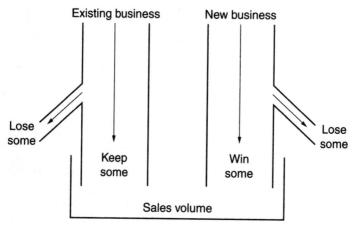

Figure 9.1 Existing and new business

Purposeful promotion is designed not only to maintain the level of sales but also increase it. Promotion is the means by which businesses communicate the benefits of their products/services to actual and potential customers. In a marketing sense, any method of communicating with customers is classified as 'promotion'.

Promotional methods include:

o Advertising

o Publicity

o Public Relations

o Selling

o Merchandising

o Sponsorship

o Direct mail

o Fax

o E-mail

o Exhibitions

o Promotions

As with all aspects of marketing, all promotional activities should be planned and managed.

90 per cent of the battle is what you say, 10 per cent is what medium you say it in.

Is your advertising getting results?

Yes. Last week we advertised for a night security guard and the next night we were robbed.

Many take the view that 'An advertisement, to be successful, must be seen, must be read, must be believed, must be remembered, must be acted upon.'

Selecting the right medium is crucial to delivering the message. The choice is determined by

o   the target market

o   the budget

o   the objectives of the promotional campaign.

The Target Market

Knowing precisely which market advertising is aimed at attracting can be traced back to how and on what basis the market is segmented. The demographic choices (e.g. gender, age, socio-economic group, lifestyle status, etc., are key variables in developing an identikit of the 'ideal customer'. Segmenting the market in this manner can prove instrumental in deciding which newspapers, magazines, journals, and other print media a particular market segment purchase.

The Budget

Advertising budgets are generally based on a crude but widespread practice of allocating around 3–4 per cent of the previous year's turnover. Allocating that resource makes for hard choices, given the demands that may be known and the unknown demands (hence a contingency sum made by prudent operators).

The Objectives of the Promotional Campaign

Advertisements aim either to inform, persuade or reassure. Informative advertisements are designed to acquaint customers with a product, service, or enterprise. Persuasive advertisements aim to influence buying behaviour by encouraging customers to buy. Reassurance advertisements are directed at maintaining customer confidence and reducing cognitive dissonance (i.e. a state of psychological tension when a choice has to be made between two equally attractive, or equally unpleasant, alternatives). An advertisement may incorporate elements of all three forms.

Creating customer awareness is automatically achieved provided the advert is read, but the ultimate purpose of an advertisement is to increase sales. In the crowded jungle of the printed word, advertisements compete to be read, which is hardly surprising considering that advertisements constitute over 70 per cent of some newspapers and magazines.

The more attractive the advertisement, the greater the likelihood of the reader's notoriously low attention span scanning it. In a determined effort to induce a person to read, advertisers use the mnemonic AIDA:

Stage	Means	Method
Attention	Gained by	o Colour o Humour o Design Appeal o Original/Unusual Copy o Size
Interest	Held by	o State Major Claim o Stress Unique Selling Point o Proposition
Desire	Created by	o Advantages o Build up
Action	What the customer must do now	o Coupons o Tear-off slips o Buy now – call in o Phone up and book

The following outline advertising table is a useful guide to help clarify the issues surrounding an advertisement. The rhetorical questions apply equally when considering radio, TV or the internet as an advertising medium.

Question	Factors to consider	Locating the answer
WHAT?	○ The product itself ○ Service ○ Special events/activities ○ Benefits/attractions of establishment	○ Result of market research ○ Internal affairs/problems ○ What the customer is really looking for – (Psychology!)
WHO?	○ Existing, or potential customers, or both ○ Age, sex, salary range ○ Social environment ○ Present/future needs ○ Likely buyers	○ Analysis of market surveys ○ Personal knowledge of customer motivation ○ What appeals to whom? ○ Are these the customers to whom I want to appeal?
WHY?	○ Profitability ○ Increased share of market ○ Keeping in the public eye ○ Creating increased interest ○ Notifying changes/new ventures in operation	○ What results are expected? ○ How best achieved in relation to cost? ○ Link back to what and whom
WHEN?	○ How to achieve maximum impact ○ Timing, e.g. morning or evening press ○ Monday or weekend ○ Not too soon, not too late	○ When do I want them to buy? ○ Is there time to see, understand and act?
WHERE?	○ Where do my customers circulate? ○ What do they read, watch? ○ Where do they pass by, spend spare time? ○ Consider cost effectiveness of media	○ Personal knowledge of customers and areas ○ Observation and questioning ○ Media research and choice
HOW?	○ Build on facts and logic, but ally to creativity ○ Appeal to the real needs of the customer, e.g. not only food/drink but companionship, rest and atmosphere	○ Appropriate to situation but outlining benefits, attractions, special features that appeal to your type and style of customer

Creativity in Marketing

Marketing is not a precise science and therefore there are few 'right answers' to marketing problems. This leaves great scope for creativity, particularly in the way a business chooses to use the various factors which influence the buying decision.

Creative marketing can also often stimulate latent demand for the product and/or services of the business as the following example (seen in the window of a restaurant in Puerto Rico) illustrates:

COME IN AND EAT OR WE'LL BOTH STARVE!

Or the following message on a blackboard outside a restaurant in Cumbria, which intrigued all who saw it.

Two weeks later all was revealed when the missing letters were added:

A city-centre hotel in the north-west of England made a considerable impact on its mid-week business accommodation occupancy figures by means of a little lateral thinking, which produced an unexpected bonus. Research done by the front desk indicated that accommodation bookings were made by secretaries, almost none of whom had ever visited the hotel, let alone seen what sort of hotel room they were booking on behalf of their bosses.

The hotel placed an advertisement, in shorthand, in the local evening paper, inviting all secretaries to an open evening.

The response was astounding. So many secretaries turned up that the hotel was almost overwhelmed. The aim was to show the bedrooms and suites, but such was the interest in all the hotel's facilities that a follow-up evening was arranged to show the conference and meeting rooms.

Not only did occupancy figures rise but demand for the meeting rooms also improved. Secretaries may not be direct users but in this case, they were certainly key influencers.

Seeking influence and forming opinion was the strategy used by a new hotel keen to establish itself among its competitors in London. Black-cab drivers were invited to a free buffet and an evening's entertainment. The event went down extremely well and put the hotel firmly on the map in the eyes of the taxi drivers, a key source of referral bookings.

This idea was first used in 1961 by Loew's Motor Hotel in New York (363 rooms), and attracted 6,513 cab drivers.

Quantifying the goodwill generated by such an event can never be accurately calculated, but the city's loquacious cab drivers never had a bad word to say about that hotel.

The only constraint to attract attention is the limit of one's imagination. Fortunately, hospitality operators seem blessed with an abundance of this.

Public Relations

*'There is only one thing in the world worse than being
talked about, and that is not being talked about!'*

OSCAR WILDE

Public relations (PR) is the establishing and maintaining of good
relations between an organization and its customers.

The role of PR is to maintain and enhance the image of the
business which is achieved in a proactive manner by creating
customer awareness, establishing brand loyalty and combating
increased competition.

A hospitality enterprise can generate relationships with its
public through a variety of means, but needs the conduits of radio,
television and the press to enhance the publicity value.

Opportunities abound for hotels to create positive PR for
themselves though special events such as exhibitions, themed
weekends, gastronomic events, conferences, and VIP guests –
all of which focus attention on attractions at, or within the hotel.

Skilful PR can also bring into focus the name of the
hotel at events away from the location. Occasional articles or a
column in the local paper, involvement with the local community
through presentation of awards at schools or colleges, radio and
television interviews, talks to local associations (e.g. rotary clubs,
townswomen's guild) are all examples of this.

Once started, PR can take on a life of its own and create
demands that justify the appointment of a full-time professional
to manage the function.

Publicity

Publicity often stems directly from public relations activity and
is usually referred to as 'free' advertising. However, although the
media exposure may not have cost anything, good publicity
demands sustained effort on the part of hospitality operators and
incurs cost and time. Adverse or unfavourable publicity can swiftly

All publicity is good publicity.

Robert, the dynamic general manager of a hotel/leisure complex, inspired all the staff to go the extra mile. He was expected to become a director of the company which owned the complex within four years of being appointed. It was no mean operation: a 200-bedroom hotel, with wildlife park, tennis and squash courts, a swimming pool, fitness gym, sauna, health studio, sports therapy – one of the most comprehensive complexes in the south of England.

Such a large operation demanded a high public profile, and his natural talents as a self-publicist meant that the business was frequently featured in the local weekly newspaper, and frequently in the regional evening paper.

Revenue increased, costs were tightly controlled, staff turnover was low, the quality of various 'products' was high, and guest satisfaction levels were exceptional. All was going swimmingly for Robert, his family and his future.

A moment of summer madness broke up his marriage and ruined his career. Allegations of an off-duty romp with female guests in the jacuzzi merited a brief paragraph in the local paper, then a quarter-page in the regional paper, and a whole page in a national Sunday paper.

Try telling Robert that all publicity is good publicity.

alter the public's perception of a company or product. Reputations that have taken years of painstaking work to achieve can be destroyed overnight through bad publicity.

More often than not, PR is seen as a reactive function to combat bad publicity, through damage limitation exercises.

Summary

o A business always needs new customers.

o Promotion includes advertising, publicity, public relations, selling, merchandising, sponsorship, direct mail, fax, e-mail, exhibitions, promotions.

o Advertising seeks to influence customer behaviour.

o AIDA is the bedrock for most print advertisements.

o Creativity is not the sole preserve of professional copywriters.

o Public relations is about good relationships.

o Publicity is free advertising.

It's the sizzle that sells the steak.

Restaurant staff are either *order takers* or *order makers*.

Service crews at Burger King, McDonald's and Kentucky Fried Chicken and other national fast food operations are encouraged to suggest at least one extra menu item to the 'grab and go' fast food clientele when they place an order. The crews are trained as *order makers*, and the high sales volume reflects this approach.

Point of Sale

'Waiter, what is the soup of the day?'
'I'll just go and find out.'

Marketing is not complete until it is continued through to the point of sale. Thorough market research, producing a product in line with the results of such research, ensuring product availability and creating a demand for it are all part of the marketing function. It is also incumbent upon any hospitality enterprise to make sure that the business is in a position to turn that demand into a sale.

Customer Expectations

At the point of sale itself customers expect:

o An enjoyable product (drink, meal, etc) at an appropriate price

o Prompt and efficient service

o Courtesy and a feeling of importance

o Comfort and relaxation

o Guidance in choice

o Understanding of their wishes and needs

Customers' expectations are met through:

o The product itself – quality, quantity, presentation, price

o The service – timing and speed to suit the market, efficiency, expertise of staff, appearance and social skills of staff

o The product support – décor, display, heating, lighting, linen, glasses, cutlery, cleanliness, etc., must all support the product

The importance of meeting customers' expectations, even exceeding them, cannot be emphasized strongly enough. It is not only much easier to increase sales to existing customers than it is to win new ones, but existing customers are more valuable. It costs about five times as much to win a new customer as it does to keep an existing one. Cost aside, replacing 1000 customers with 1000 new customers is not the straight trade that it may seem, because the lost customers may give the company a bad reputation and make it harder to bring in the new ones.

The Selling Process

'Selling is making people want what you have got, while marketing is selling people what they want.'

Selling is simplicity itself. The process involves just two individuals:

The customer: has needs and wants

The salesperson: has knowledge of the products and services

The aim of the process is to achieve as high a degree of overlap of the circles, and the onus falls on the sales person to achieve that. Selling successfully depends on the salesperson to:

o   Discover the customer's needs and unearth latent ones

o   Demonstrate how the product or service will benefit the customer by satisfying those needs

By following the process in that order the two circles will merge – the higher the degree of overlap the more satisfied the customer is likely to be.

Customer needs

Product benefits

Trying to achieve a total eclipse is a waste of effort without the salesperson conducting a conversation which

- o enables the salesperson to discover the customer's needs

- o encourages the customer to clarify those needs for themselves

The skills of questioning and active listening are vital if the salesperson is to:

- o be able to recall information about the product and service

- o describe how the features of the product match the customer's needs

- o demonstrate how the product or service will benefit the customer

This structure enables the salesperson to sell benefits, and there is a high correlation between selling benefits to making successful sales.

Selling to customers in the hospitality industry is made much easier as, in most cases, they have already made a positive decision by entering the hotel, restaurant, pub or club. When a customer is on the seller's territory, the seller is at a distinct advantage.

Staff owe their appointment to the skill and ability to do the job they were engaged for, whether as a conference and banqueting porter, barman, waitress, leisure attendant, or receptionist.

Front-of-house staff in direct daily contact with customers are not employed solely to sell the products and services of the hotel, they are employed to *give customers an opportunity to buy* those products and services. This is distinct from the high pressure sales techniques more associated with the double glazing industry.

Giving customers the opportunity to buy means ensuring the availability of items and information, it means ensuring that employees know the products and services available, it means instilling a cultural zeal to satisfy, delight, and exceed customer expectations.

The following instructions from a buyer apply to employees in direct contact with customers, just as much as to the sales personnel to whom they are more purposefully directed.

I am a Buyer

1. I dislike being called 'Mr Er' or 'Mr Um'. I am proud of my name and I like the salesperson to use it. If they cannot discover it, worm it out of someone, ask me for it; if they don't they aren't a salesperson anyway, and I'd rather they didn't waste my time.

2. Start talking about *me*. I like myself, my family, my business and my profits. I don't necessarily like you, your family, or your business.

3. Sometimes I arouse my own interest in a hotel by talking about it; give me a chance to speak, and then listen to me.

4. Find out all my needs. You may be barking up the wrong tree.

5. Never take me for granted. Fight as hard for my business at each call you make upon me as you did when you first dealt with me, otherwise you will let your competitors in.

6. Find out about your voice. I am a little hard of hearing, but I don't like to be shouted at. Practise voice production, so that I can understand what you are talking about.

7. Don't try to persuade me by a spate of words. I might sign your order, but I will probably think better of it later, and cancel it. Convince me by facts and we shall both be happy.

8. Tell me the truth, and keep your promises.

9. Be optimistic. I know all the bad news without you telling it to me.

10. Be warm and kindly, not just an unsympathetic parrot. I can get all the information I want from a brochure. I need you to make the words live.

11. Ask my advice. Make me feel important. If you talk down to me I shall kick you right out.

12. Be well-mannered and friendly, but not too friendly.

13. For goodness' sake don't talk-talk-talk. Please ease up now and again.

14. I don't like buying from a grubby salesperson. Do me a favour and look, right now, at your fingernails, hair and shoes – and don't forget to brush that suit before you visit me.

15. If it is raining I don't object to you carrying an umbrella. But don't rest it in my room so that puddles of water form on my floor.

16. If I am to make up my mind I want to hear the whole story. Don't cut your sales sequence, even if I appear to be disinterested. That is my act for putting off weak salespeople. I reckon that if a salesperson can be put off easily they haven't much faith in their hotel. And if they haven't, why should I have?

17. Don't waste my time by telling me funny stories. I rarely laugh at stage comedians, and what makes you think that you are funnier than the professionals?

18. Know your sales aids. I don't appreciate fumblers, and the 'I'll find it in a minute' salesperson.

19. Remember, there is only one thing more contagious than enthusiasm and that is the lack of it.

20. Let me feel, when you leave me, that I have a friend – that you will never let me down. And do nothing to jeopardize the good opinion I have formed of you.

Types of Sales Activity

Sales activity is split between *internal* and *external; direct* and *indirect*, as featured in Figure 11.1, together with some examples.

	Direct	**Indirect**

Internal	Face-to-face
	Promotional
	  leaflets
	Sales literature
		Merchandise
		  items
		Signs
		Displays

External	Personal sales pitches Direct mail shots Telephone selling Exhibitions Brochures	Consortia Booking agencies Tourist boards Guide books Feature articles

Figure 11.1 Types of sales activity

Merchandising

It used to be a popular sport of guests to purloin souvenirs from hotels of distinction. Ashtrays, cruets, tableware, bath robes, stationery, even sheets and pillowcases, nothing was sacred to the light-fingered customers keen to display mementos to family and friends.

The 'rape and pillage' of hotel stocks by guests is alarming, but some hotels recognize it by pricing their 'wares' and putting them on display. The result: increased sales and no more furtive guests anxious to conceal their 'trophies'.

Turning 'leakage' into a merchandising opportunity by default may be opportunist but it certainly solved an embarrassing dilemma for a renowned hotel in Scotland.

Merchandising is the psychological persuasion at the point of sale, designed to trigger a buying reaction from the customer. It has also been called 'Exposing products to the danger of being sold'.

The objective of marketing is to maximize opportunities to sell to customers by making products and services easily available to them.

Although a business is an external advertisement in its own right, promoting and silently selling itself by virtue of its physical presence, the exterior is merchandised through signs, illuminations and exterior lighting. This cumulative effect creates an image to customers.

Once inside, care must be taken to ensure the customers' attention is caught by clear signs pointing them to the products and services available.

Merchandising Areas

These may include restaurants and bars, lounges, dining areas, coffee shops, lifts, corridors, bedrooms, bathrooms, even the smallest room!

Use space creatively such as counters, shelves, lift interiors and other walled areas where people congregate, otherwise known as 'hot spots'.

Merchandising items include: signs and tent cards, leaflets, menus, brochures, notices and wine list displays.

Merchandising alone is useful. It is even more effective when it is co-ordinated and themed to build an image. However, its power is really felt when 'Effective merchandising is linked to staff who are trained and motivated to sell'.

Sponsorship

The means and methods of sponsorship vary greatly from direct financial support of a sporting team, or individuals, to the provision of community facilities, such as playground equipment for children or litter bins in the immediate vicinity of the business. The purpose of sponsorship is to foster goodwill and enhance the image of the business, especially if it is associated with improvements to the environment.

Building relations with the community can reap rewards. A hotel in Shropshire bought the football strip for a local team of 10–14-year-old boys. This gesture brought untold goodwill and generated unexpected publicity in the local paper when the team came top of the league two years later.

Direct Mail

Direct mail is sales literature delivered to an address and includes letters, flyers, brochures and leaflets. It is used to generate new customers, maintain the loyalty of existing customers and renew the interest of lapsed customers. Each group obviously warrants a separately tailored message. Considerable copy writing skills are needed to grab the attention of recipients, as much of the huge quantity of unsolicited mail is termed junk and discarded without ever being opened.

Increasingly sophisticated databases means that potential as well as existing customers can be specifically targeted. So instead of using the blunderbuss approach of peppering a mile-wide target an inch deep, use a rifle to focus on an inch wide target and penetrate it a mile deep.

Facsimile

The problem often encountered by direct mail shots is the envelope. There is no guarantee that the envelope will be opened by the addressee and the contents read by the named individual. A fax can overcome this barrier.

Electronic Mail

E-mail is currently the most personable form of promotion. Addressees have been 'conditioned' to read all e-mail messages before saving, printing or deleting them.

Exhibitions

Being seen to have 'a presence in the market place' can be achieved by booking space at an exhibition or travel show. Hotels in particular have found that the cost of taking exhibition space can prove rewarding not only in generating new enquiries and contacts, but in converting a significant proportion of those enquiries into sales.

Promotion

Local, regional or national events and notable calendar days provide positive opportunities for hospitality enterprises to generate interest and increase sales. Large-scale events can involve a consortium of vested interest groups, such as airline and coach operators, local tourist boards, retail shops, heritage sites, etc., to maximize impact for a significant event.

Summary

- o Successful selling depends on meeting customer needs
- o Customers have latent needs
- o Customers buy benefits
- o Selling is an activity undertaken directly, indirectly, in house or externally
- o Merchandising is a form of silent selling
- o Sponsorship can generate community loyalty
- o Direct mail needs to be targeted to be effective
- o Faxes are open to be read
- o E-mails cannot be ignored
- o Exhibitions are a platform to promote
- o Promotions are singular events to stimulate interest and demand

In the American Mid-west, cowboys took a red-hot iron to the buttocks of cattle to imprint the name of their ranch. Branding cattle established ownership and clearly marked them out from neighbours' herds.

A brand name can evoke perceptions by customers; some may be positive, others less so. For instance,

o Aston Martin suggests status and prestige

o Ferrari is synonymous with speed

o Skoda is associated with low running costs

These are all cars but their name alone suggests an image which affects how customers perceive their worth.

Hospitality enterprises attempt to differentiate their product from competitors by establishing brand names. Successful ones achieve high customer loyalty whereas new ones have to attract customers:

Pizzaland

Holiday Inn

Kentucky Fried Chicken

Hyatt Regency

Travel Lodge

These are all brand names, users of which know the range of products offered at each and every unit, the prices charged, the style of service given, and the level of quality. In short, the customer knows exactly what to expect irrespective of the location and, perhaps more reassuringly, knows there are no unpleasant surprises in store.

An established brand name can offer a haven of reassuring cognitive comfort to the weary traveller, the hungry tourist, or the anxious holidaymaker. Sophisticates may identify this (state of) mental anguish as cognitive dissonance, which an established brand name can do much to reduce.

Imitation is said to be the sincerest form of flattery and those who 'invented' products first have been flattered many times over by new entrants to the market. The result is brand wars:

o Coca-Cola versus Pepsi

o Guinness versus Murphy's

o Hilton versus Sheraton versus Marriott versus Hyatt Regency

o McDonald's versus Burger King

Summary

A brand name is like a designer label: identifiable with certain attributes.

13 CUSTOMERS

The sign on a reception desk in a hideaway in Devon says it all – 'We are as happy to welcome all our guests as we are to see some depart.'

What Are Customers?

Customers are not dependent upon us, we depend upon them for our living;

Customers are people who come to us because they need certain services;

Customers are the most important people in this firm, whether they come in person, write to us, telephone, e-mail or fax us;

Customers are not statistics, they are flesh and blood human beings, with emotions and prejudices just like ours;

Customers are not an interruption to our work, they are the very purpose of it;

Customers are not people with whom we should argue – to win an argument is to lose a customer;

Without customers there *is* no business.

From a marketing viewpoint, it is important to consider the needs and requirements of customers for at least three major reasons:

1. People do not buy goods and services for what they are – they buy them for what they do for them.

2. Understanding what makes people tick and why they buy things makes it far more likely one will be able to satisfy those needs.

3. If a group of customers display similar behaviours and have similar needs, they form a market segment. It is far easier, and more profitable, to supply a common range of goods and services to a group segment than to a wide-ranging set of individuals.

One particular approach to people's needs, which fits the hospitality industry very well, was advanced by a behavioural scientist called Abraham Maslow in 1943. He proposed a hierarchy of needs consisting of five levels:

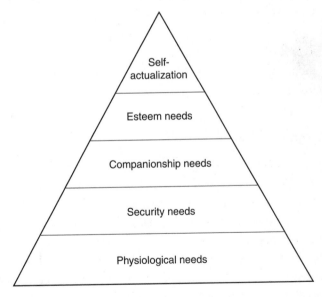

Figure 13.1 Maslow's hierarchy of needs

Maslow's premise is that all of us have needs which require satisfying in ascending order, i.e. higher-level needs only emerge as those immediately preceding are satisfied.

At the base of the triangle are physiological needs of food and drink, necessary for survival. At the next level are the needs of safety and security, represented by the stability of a home, a job and freedom from anxiety.

Then come the needs for love, companionship and a sense of belonging. This whole area of needs is central to the hospitality industry whether it's a case of providing an intimate family meal for four or a celebration for a victorious sports team.

After that is the need for esteem and status. The hospitality industry caters to the egos of its customers as much as to their stomachs, and with some justification. Many people are hungrier for recognition than they are for food and drink alone. Warm, friendly greetings and the appropriate use of customers' names do much to reinforce their esteem and accord them the status they seek.

The need for self-actualization, the desire for self-fulfilment or being the best you can, can be met through activity breaks, featuring special interest groups – fishing, golf, antique master-classes, painting, hot air ballooning. Whatever a person's hobby or interests, most activities can be catered for by hotels over the course of a year.

Customer Care

Most businesses lose 25 per cent of their customers annually and yet most companies spend five times as much on generating new customers as on retaining existing ones.

Customer satisfaction or dissatisfaction comes more and more from the way the person is treated. Improved technology, more affluence, greater sophistication, foreign travel, intense competition all play their part in increasing customers' expectations of levels of service.

Customer care is about caring for customers and caring about them. Customer care is a skill; therefore it can be learnt; therefore staff can be trained.

96 per cent of dissatisfied customers
do not go back and complain

They tell 7 other people of their experience

10% will tell at least 20 others

90% will never return

It costs 5 times as much to attract a new customer
as it does to keep an existing one.

The figures and percentages for dissatisfied customers are frightening, and the consequences of failure to meet customer expectations are disastrous. All the marketing effort employed from assiduous research of the 3Cs, not to mention the planning and implementation of the 4Ps, is imperilled at the point of delivery of the product if the service proves inadequate.

Some of the key characteristics of customer care are:

o Knowledgeable and professional conduct

o Friendly and courteous, even when under pressure

o Helpful but not pushy

o Good emphatic listeners, and caring

o Willing to take responsibility or blame

o Do what they said they will

o Keep customers informed, without chasing

o Give prompt response to an enquiry

o Take pride in company, products of service

o Give a friendly smile

It takes around 17 facial muscles to smile and around 68 to frown. Not only is a smile less work for the face, it also helps to disarm customer complainants – justified or otherwise!

There is a virtuous circle between delivering superior customer value and profit levels; the reward for consistently superior value is high customer loyalty and retention.

Summary

o Customer care is a skill.

o Customers are not all born dissatisfied.

o Customer complaints give an opportunity to satisfy customers.

o Customers' needs vary.

o Some customers are hungrier for recognition than for food and drink alone.

'Today is the tomorrow that was yesterday.'

Tomorrow never comes but the future is here today, as the development of plastic cards illustrates. Credit cards are 1960s technology, carrying only a few hundred characters – enough for your name and account number. Smart cards are 1980s technology with little chips built in – enough to hold a page of text.

Ultracards are the technology of the new century; the magnetic strip on the back can hold the contents of a novel. Prototypes are expected to hold 200 times that amount.

Technological advances with plastic are being matched by mobile phones. First there was analogue, then there was digital, and now there is 3G (third generation). These have Wireless Application Protocol (WAP), which means the internet is accessible through the mobile phone.

From a marketing perspective this means hospitality operators place a much greater emphasis on the style, format, information and ease of use of their web site. Just as some hotel brochures excite and delight the imagination, others suggest the hotel is caught in a time warp; these perceptions will be reflected in the design of web sites.

Once you had to be computer-literate; now you have to be network literate. The internet is the vehicle for all the information travelling around the world in a multimedia fashion through the World Wide Web.

Hotels, stuck with that most perishable of all items, the unsold bedroom, may offer it on line to customers who are aware that competitor hotels also have unsold rooms and can therefore dictate the price they are willing to pay. The customer may be seen as more than just a king of consumerism; he will be lord of all he surveys on the internet.

The popularity of a web site is easily established by the number of hits it receives – an accurate evaluation of the effectiveness of advertising. Creating sophisticated designs of the sites will be a vital factor in generating enquiries that lead to sales, and e-commerce will become an increasingly important method of conducting business transactions. Hard copy brochures, leaflets and menus may diminish as the use of technology becomes more dominant.

Touch screen menus featuring a hotel's facilities – describing bedrooms, conference facilities, menu dishes, wine lists – and the facility to translate that information instantly to the native language of the customer will eradicate misunderstandings.

Future technology – its prospects and use in the hospitality industry – will strengthen the relationship between buyer and seller. This new concept – relationship marketing – seeks to embrace and enhance the relationships with customers. This will be strengthened further as more accurate information on customer purchases and spending power will enable hospitality enterprises to assess the significance of their key customer database.

In 1906 Vilfredo Pareto advanced a theory of unequal distribution suggesting that a small percentage of characteristics always applies to a high percentage of the overall population. This has become known as the Pareto principle or the '80/20 rule' and can be readily applied to a wide range of issues. For example 80 per cent of customers account for 20 per cent of sales and 80 per cent of sales are provided by 20 per cent of customers. The implication of the 80/20 rule is to concentrate effort on the vital few.

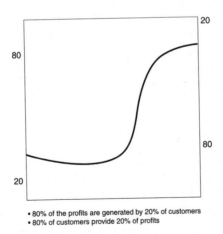

- 80% of the profits are generated by 20% of customers
- 80% of customers provide 20% of profits

Figure 14.1 The Pareto principle

CONCLUSIONS

Marketing is much more than selling and advertising; it is concerned with identifying customer needs and wants and selecting those areas which a hospitality business can satisfy successfully.

It is about measuring the market demand and examining competitors' activities.

It is about setting objectives, developing strategies and using creatively those various factors that influence customers to buy.

It is about measuring the results of marketing activity and continuously reviewing the ever-changing needs in the market place.

A Few Final Thoughts

Customers go out to eat in **restaurants**, yet some hotels still have dining-rooms which remain half-empty. Why *is* that?

Most customers sleep under **duvets** at home, yet most hotels use sheets, blankets and eiderdowns.

Time spent waiting for someone, or something, always seems twice as long as it actually is.

The art of hospitality is to make people feel at home when you wish they were.

USEFUL ADDRESSES

Industry Organizations

Brewers and Licensed Retailers Association, 42 Portman Square, London W1H 0BB

British Hospitality Association, Queens House, 55–96 Lincoln's Inn Fields, London WC2A 3BH

British Tourist Authority, Thames Tower, Blacks Road, Hammersmith, London W6 9EL

Catering Managers Association of Great Britain and Channel Islands, Mount Pleasant, Egton, Whitby, Yorkshire YO21 1UE

Cookery and Food Association, 1 Victoria Parade, 331 Sandycombe Road, Richmond, Surrey TW9 3NB

Tourism Society, 26 Chapter Street, London SW1P 4ND

Vegetarian Society, Parkdale, Dunham Road, Altrincham, Cheshire WA14 4QG

Educational Organizations

British Institute of Innkeeping, 42 Portman Square, London W1H 0BB

Chartered Institute of Marketing, Moor Hall, Cookham, Berkshire SL6 9QH

Council for Hospitality Management Education, 26 Birtley Rise, Bramley, Guildford, Surrey GU5 0HZ

Hospitality Training Foundation, International House, 7 High Street, Ealing, London W5 5DB

Hotel Catering and International Management Association, 191 Trinity Road, London SW17 7HN

Institute of Leisure & Amenity Management, ILAM House, Lower Basildon, Reading RG8 9NE

Institute of Travel & Tourism, 113 Victoria Street, St Albans, Hertfordshire AL1 3TJ

Market Research Society, 15 Northburn Street, London EC1V 0AH

Restaurant Association, African House, 64–78 Kingsway, London WC2B 6AH

Wine and Spirit Education Trust, 5 Kings House, 1 Queen Street Place, London EC4R 1QS

REFERENCES

Ansoff, Igor H. (1975)
Corporate Strategy,
Harmondsworth: Penguin.

Buttle, F. (1984) *Hotel and Food Services Marketing: A Managerial Approach*. London: Cassell.

HCIMA (2000) Yearbook: *Food Service Intelligence*.

Hospitality Training Foundation (1996) *Key Facts and Figures*.

Jones, Peter and Andrew Lockwood (1989)
The Management of Hotel Operations, London: Cassell.

Kotler, P. (1997)
Marketing Management 9th Edition, Prentice Hall Inc.

Lundberg, D.E.,
The Tourist Business, New York: Van Nostrand Reinhold.

Murdick, R., Render, B. and Russell, R. (1990)
Service Operations Management, Boston: Allyn and Bacon.

National Office of Statistics Report (1998) *Social Focus on Older People*, London: HMSO.

Roberts, J. (1993) *Marketing for the Hospitality Industry*, London: Hodder and Stoughton.

Rogers, E.M. (1992)
The Diffusion of Innovations, New York: The Free Press.

Weaver, N. and Morris, A. (1994) *Hospitality Marketing*, London: Butterworth and Heinemann.

INDEX